DIANA R: MY JOURNEY

"A TRUE STORY"

by

Johann Stirner

and

Diana Berrios Reyes

DORRANCE
PUBLISHING CO
EST. 1920
PITTSBURGH, PENNSYLVANIA 15238

Dorrance Publishing Co
585 Alpha Drive
Pittsburgh, PA 15238
Visit our website at *www.dorrancebookstore.com*

ISBN: 978-1-6366-1200-3
EISBN: 978-1-6366-1790-9

DIANA R:
MY JOURNEY

"A TRUE STORY"

INTRODUCTION

 This documentary is about the life and journey of a little girl and her desperate mother. From El Salvador to the United States.

They now live in Los Angeles area. They are illegal and have to take their chances one day at the time. They both are working for a living. Diana is not a little girl anymore. She got her High School Diploma. She is now working at day time; in the evening hours she goes to school to become a legal aide. Her mother goes to evening school to be a physio therapist. In El Salvador she was a certified nurse so she is in a familiar territory. Both learned English and are fluent, at least since I met them.

I am from Norway, so I am the lucky one because I can travel free and on one of my many journeys, I met many interesting people. Diana and her mother are two of them. It is interesting to realize what difference a background made. I was fortunate to grow up in a politically stable surrounding. Free education and the possibility of worldwide travel. Diana and her mother were not that lucky. They grew up in a different environment, having to fight for everything, and at the end, their surroundings turned so life-threatening that they had to leave their home and even Diana had to leave her sister behind and for her mother her oldest daughter just to save themselves.

I was lucky to meet up with them. We are from different continents, and since I met them, I was looking for the differences between them and me. At least this is what the politicians in Washington try to make us believe. I did not find any difference. Instead I realized how much we had in common.

ONE MORNING

This story began when I promised to help out a friend. He had a business selling propane gas and was shorthanded. We knew each other for a long time and I had free time, so I gladly offered my help.

Most of the customers were food trucks who needed the propane for their cooking. The majority of these trucks where staffed by two people; one did the cooking and other the driving and collecting the money. The majority of them were staffed by ladies; only some of them had a man as driver, but as far as I could tell, the cook was always a lady. In this business you can only make a living if you don't mind long work hours, so this crew usually worked ten to twelve hours, five to six days a week. Because I filled their tanks and these ladies were in their forties or older, I was kind of surprised when one of the new customers I got, was a little girl driving one of the big trucks.

She must at least be eighteen years old and have a license but couldn't possibly be much older. Her age and appearance were different from the other lady customers I served. Sure, she was new and, as always with new customers, she was not familiar with the area or driving this big truck. She definitely needed help, both to turn around and to back up, before I was able to fill her tank with propane. It did not take long, maybe three to four weeks, and this little lady caught up and did not require any special attention from me anymore. She turned into a regular customer fast and an easy one too.

One day I was able to ask her how she learned to know about our place, because many of the new food trucks ladies start filling in the company where they park at night. It was easier for them to get around until they catch up with the price difference and start filling with me. I asked her how she found our place; she told me that her mom was my customer too and she told her that it was cheaper here and how to find us. I was glad that my service was appreciated and the next day when her mother came in, I thanked her for that.

DIANA

A couple of weeks later by one of the refill visits, which were already a routine by now, her truck did not start. I tried to help her. We checked all the connections to and from the battery but nothing. According to my instructions, that was all I was allowed to do, so the plan for a situation like this is to push the food truck into the back of the yard so that it is out of the way until the field mechanic can come. With a dead engine there is no servo steering, so the little girl was not able to steer the truck by herself; I had to do the pushing as well as to help her turn the steering wheel. It was hard work, much too hard for a little girl.

It took us about twenty minutes, but finally we got the truck in the back of the yard. We made sure the break was on and everything else secured and off. She then tried to get in touch with the field mechanic, who was contracted to serve this company. It was still early in the morning and dark. I told her to wait at my station; at least there was light and a place to sit and she had my company. I introduced myself and she told me that her name was Diana. She also told me her mother's name.

I knew immediately where to place her mom, sure she was my customer too. These early morning hours can be boring. There is a waiting time between the different food trucks to come in and get filled up. We had time to talk, and because she looked so young, I asked her how old she was. When she told me that she is twenty years old, I was not surprised. She told me also when she finished high school, she started going to college in the evening to get an education, but from 3:30 in the morning, she is working, driving this food truck.

The money pays for school and helps her mom with the daily expenses. In the meantime, daylight was slowly replacing the darkness of the night, and I was able to see her for the first time outside her food truck. She was really tiny but a very pretty girl. She asked me whether I wanted something to eat because her cook was already at work in the truck to prepare the different meals for the day. It was still too early for me to eat, but I would gladly have some coffee if she had it. She went and came back with coffee and some cookies and we sat down to have a little pre-breakfast, waiting for the field mechanic.

In my experience that takes time. These trucks are on average about twenty years old, and the owners usually have many trucks, therefore these mechanics are very busy. These ladies only work the food trucks. They have nothing to do with service or repair.

It was still early and as usual I am not busy at this hour, so I was curious about this little girl and I asked her how she ended up doing this kind of work. Well her mom worked for the same company, so it was easy for her to get work there too. I got impressed, not only because these food trucks ladies work long hours, but this little girl had to go to school after work; she must have sixteen-hour days.

She was pleasant to talk too and not shy, I guess because her mom was my longtime customer too. Previously her mom had told me that they were from El Salvador, so I asked her when and how they got to the US. She smiled at me and asked: "Do you really want to know this story? It will take a while." Knowing we had a couple of hours, at least, until the store formally opened or the mechanic arrived, I wanted to hear it. Why not? The only interruption we could expect were the other food trucks filling propane, which did not take more than three to four minutes each.

ZACAMIL - SAN SALVADOR

She took another look at me, but after a moment of thinking, she started telling me: The history of my mom and me moving to the United States started seven years ago, in a part of San Salvador which is called Zacamil. My mother had a house there, not in an expensive area, but not bad either. It was an okay neighborhood. The people where friendly and the neighbors knew and helped each other. It was a decent place, the house had one big room downstairs and three rooms on the second floor, which my mom had added over time. We lived there with my older sister. She was six years older than me and was a nice girl, had a boyfriend and went to a Christian school.

I was the problem. I was not a nice girl, even if I went to the same Christian school, but besides fighting with the teachers, I was also fighting with my mother all the time. I always wanted to have it my way. But my real problems started outside home and school one day. I had to walk from home to school, the same road every day ever since I was nine years old. My mom was working, so I walked by myself to get to and home from school.

My walk went exactly between the 13th and the 18th district in Zacamil, as this part in San Salvador was called. The two districts were controlled by two rival gangs, the 13th gang and the 18th gang. Both gangs had their bases close to the road where I had to walk every day. Usually, if you walk the road fast, dressed in your Christian school uniform they did not bother you, but you had to stick to yourself, stay kind of neutral, not talking to one of the gangs or the other and certainly do not affiliate with one or the other, because if you do, you attract their interest, or worse you could turn into their property.

I can't say how far the word property can be defined in this matter, but if you affiliate with one side in any way, you are automatically the enemy of the other gang. I was a wild kind of child in these early teenage years. I liked to challenge everybody and to the big concern of my mother, I started to hang out with the 13th gang. Over time, they started to give me the attention I admired and wanted. I started to witness how they threatened people and extorted money by intimidating them. I also saw how they rob other people of their money and belongings, by putting guns to their heads or beating them up. Instead of being disgusted by their behavior, I was impressed and wanted to be a part of it. This had consequences, it made me a target for the 18th and other competing gangs.

Almost every week there were shootings, often somebody got hit and many times one of their own. They knew that my mom worked in a hospital, therefore they came to me and asked to get my mom. She was a certified nurse. She removed the bullets, disinfected and sewed the bullet holes. My mom didn't like it, not only that it was illegal, but she could have lost her job in the hospital if the authorities found out. But she did it because the gang left us alone and gave me and my sister protection.

I guess this was one of the reasons the gang respected me, but each time they needed help, I had to call my mom to help them. They even paid my mom, even if she refused payment, but we could not say anything, otherwise they would kill us in a heartbeat. Sometimes when the gang settled a dispute over borderlines or other things, our neighborhood would turn into a warzone. The two gangs would start a shootout, then they carried their wounded to their headquarters, which they called their protected and barricaded buildings.

Then I had to call on my mom again and as soon as she got back from her work at the hospital, she had to take her little bag, go over, and start operating and sewing. Over time I slowly turned into a thirteen-year-old revolutionary, and a gang member, I even got my own gun.

Life was simple for me, my mom was wrong, my sister was a pussy, and I was right. I was not aware that this behavior not only created difficulties for me and my family, but it started a rivalry on the borderlines of two competing gangs because the other gang needed medical attention too. These gang members had one thing in common, they could not go to the hospital because if they would, after treatment they would go straight to jail, but they knew that my mom was able to help them. My mom never charged them, but they would always put money in her bag, as well as respect her, me, and my sister.

My sister was the complete opposite, compared to me, she was the holy one, for her it was school, church, home, and my mother. But my affiliation and behavior resulted in great danger for her too, because at one point, members of the competing gang tried to kidnap her, to force my mom to help one of their gang members, who had a bullet wound, if my mom refused the other gang could rape or kill my sister. A couple of weeks before, there was this fourteen-year-old boy. His mom had moved into our street.

I introduced him to our gang and I kind of liked him. He was nice and because he still had some contacts with some former gang members, he got knowledge about their plan and was able to warn us. With help of my gang, we were able to spoil their plans they did not get to my sister. He also started to tell us about their organization, locations and so on. One day, it was a couple of weeks later, he disappeared; we found his mutilated body on top of a pile of trash.

This situation got worse, when members of the 18th gang started following me on the way home from school and threatening me. My mother's concerns increased dramatically. That afternoon when she returned from work, she made us sit down and tried to make us understand about the consequences this could have for all of us.

These gangs made their money with illegal activities like kidnapping, drug dealing, and prostitution and our only way to survive was based on my mom helping them, but if Mom got caught by the authorities, she would lose her job and license; either way we could not win. If me or my sister got taken by one of the competing gangs, there were several options. First, I could be held for ransom. My mother had a regular job in the hospital and she owned a house. In addition, we had family members living in the United States. For these gangs this means that she was able to get money and pay ransom for me. The other possibility is that I got forced to work for them as a prostitute to make money for the gang this way.

The police knew about these gangs, but they were not helping. They feared for their own lives and the lives of their families. In Central America these gangs have influence and a long arm. My mom went to the US Embassy several times to try to get a visa for us and ask for asylum in the United States. My dad and my aunt lived there, but we were denied each time.

Ever since I was a little girl, I remembered this gang wars. The 18th gang would go and shoot members of the 13th gang and the other way around, with impunity, especially people they suspected of snitching or being affiliated with the opposite gang. To try to kill each other was the way of living for them. It was war and you had to choose a side and have your gun always ready at any given time. I was thirteen years when I earned my first gun, and I carried it all the time, when I was out of my school uniform. One time the 18th gang came over to our side on a reprisal attack and immediately open fire.

I am not sure whether they were after me again. I took cover behind the door when the shooting started, my gun in my hand, my sister ran upstairs into her room hiding under the bed. I did not need to participate in the fight, but took a glimpse through the window at times.

Everybody could get hit, even by accident, innocent or not. The guys shouted and shot it out on the street right in the front of our home. When the gunfire subsided, there were two people dead and several wounded on the street; it was a warzone.

I remember, when one of the boys in our gang screamed at me to take cover. After a while he came back and asked me to call my mom to get over here as fast as possible with her medical bag. They carried the wounded to the bunker; this was what they called the basement in their headquarters. It was more and more clear to me that I was respected mostly because they depended on my mother's help.

As usual the police stayed away, they came to our street when it was over and the street clear.

SAN MIGUELITO

When my mother came back from work, she went immediately to their headquarters, where she worked on them for several hours. When she came back that night, she looked tired, her clothes were dirty and full of blood, and she went right into the shower.

The next day, I got a written statement from school to give to my mom. The message stated that I was evicted from school because of my aggressive behavior and affiliation with gangs, which was unacceptable for a student in a Christian school. I had lost the chance for a good education.

Mom came back from work in the evening, and she still looked tired after working the night before on the wounded boys. When she started reading the letter from my school, she started crying; it was too much for her. She told me that these are the consequences of our involvement with the gang and that I am not allowed to leave the house anymore. I felt like a prisoner, I was not even allowed to step outside the front door.

About a week later, she just returned from work and I could see in her face that she had something serious in mind. She looked at me and my sister and said: "Girls we cannot continue like this, we have to move." She ordered us to start packing our belongings. She took my sister out of school too. Then, we moved to San Miguelito to my grandmother's house in another part of town. Within days, she arranged a different school where we could get from the house to school by bus.

Slowly in my mind, I began to realize that it was me and my affiliation with the gangs that were the reasons for the actions my mother had to take to protect us. Instead of living in our own house, we lived at Grandma's house. My sister, my mom, and grandma. One day, I forgot to take money with me to pay the bus fair and I had to walk home from school.

A couple of days later, I realized that somebody followed me. Members of the gangs had found out where I went and started following me to my house. I tried to lose them, but they traced me. For the security of my sister and my own, I had to tell my mom immediately. I could tell by their clothes—these were the members of the 18th gang from our old neighborhood. They were on to us. They had checked the different schools and when I forgot the money for the bus, they were able to trace me to the place where we were living now. I guessed they wanted revenge for the help we gave the other gang.

We were in grave and immediate danger, not only me but my sister and our mom too, and it put an additional strain on our situation. My mom started crying again. We were running out of options. Now, I could not leave my grandmother's house either. A couple of days later, a friend noticed that the members of the gang were looking for us right at the front entrance of my grandma's house. It will only be a matter of time that they break in to get us. At night we barricaded the front door. I will never forget this situation; my mom was very nervous, and I was not allowed to step outside the door. I had lost the privilege of going to school again, and I could not even go for a walk with my grandma. I was a prisoner again.

LEAVING

That night, our mother moved us again to another place in San Salvador, she said it was temporary she also took time off from her job in the hospital. She got busy preparing something, I did not understand at that time and she did not give me any details. For a couple of days and nights, she started to work the old sewing machine our great grandmother gave us.

Much later, I should find out she was hiding money in different places in our clothes. At the time I was not sure what she had in mind, but then she called us into the living room to have a serious talk with us. She had tears in her eyes when she told me the only option left for me was to leave, if I wanted a future. I had to get out of the country. The alternative for me was to possibly get killed, because of my young age she needed to go with me. I felt terrible that I got us in this situation, but we had no choice. We had to leave as fast as possible and leave everything behind.

The worst choice was, that my sister had to stay behind with Grandma. She was close to graduating and had already a nice and serious boyfriend. She was not a primary target for the gang, I was. My mom and me had to go and try to start over again, in a completely different place. I cried all day and night until I didn't have tears left to cry. The next morning, I talked to my mom and told her that I was ready to do whatever she decided.

Mom told me that she already talked to some friends, who had connections and recommended a "coyote" who had transported people successfully before. These coyotes transport people professionally and get them over the borders.

A couple of nights later, she woke me up. It was midnight. I remember, she was specific on how to get dressed, three pairs of panties, two pants, two shirts, other clothes, soap, pads, and even condoms in my little backpack. I was due to get my menstruation any day now, and the condoms were for the worst situation possible. In case somebody forced himself on us, we could at least try to protect ourselves. She did the same, then she took her backpack and out the door we went in the middle of the night. My sister standing at the doorstep, tears running down her face, crying, my grandma holding her and telling my mom not to worry that she was going to take care of her.

My mother was in tears, taking a final look at her oldest daughter she had to leave behind. I was paralyzed. I could only grasp what will be ahead of us. I ran back and gave my grandma a hug then my sister. I remember her last words like if it was yesterday: "Take care of my mom, I love you, and take care of yourself." That was the last time I saw my sister. I hated myself at this moment.

Little did I know, at that point, that my mother despite the short notice had everything carefully prepared. She tried to get a visa and asylum with the US embassy, three times, but was denied each time. To use a coyote was the only remaining option to get me out. The coyote she hired had organized this kind of operation before and instructed her when to be ready, how to dress, and what to take for this journey to the United States. Outside the door, there was a man and a taxi waiting for us; they drove us to a bus terminal. There we stepped into the bus, which took us all the way to the Guatemalan border. First, we had to get over this border and through this country to reach the border to Mexico and from there all the way until we reached the border of the United States.

These coyotes were making a living smuggling people. Later I realized they not only smuggled people but drugs too. If I was a little girl with a big mouth and little brain, it was at that night that I realized what trouble I had created. My mother found it necessary to take these desperate measures to get me out of our home and country leaving everything behind. My big sister, my grandma, and our house. Now I realized why she worked the last couple of days and nights to hide money in our clothes. Family and friends visiting and bringing additional money they could spare as well as saying goodbye.

She had carefully selected what we should wear not to attract attention, as she was carefully filling our backpacks with the essentials—everything in accordance to the instruction of the coyote. I remember when I wanted to take my new tennis shoes, she said it was dangerous. We used the well-worn ones, leaving the new ones behind at home. To get to the Guatemalan border was the easy part. This border is separated by a river and the only way to get over to the other side was by boat. The first challenge of the journey started right there. The coyote drove us to a farm on the riverbank. The farmer worked for him. He had a small wooden boat with an outboard engine waiting.

GUATEMALA

I remember, the boat had only space for five or six people, but beside us there were six other people waiting, with ten people in the boat, it was completely overloaded. The owner instructed us how to sit and not to put our hands or feet outside the boat, because the river was infested by gators who did not care which one of our body parts ended up in their stomach. I remember my mom was sitting and looking over to a little sandbank, on the other side, she saw a gator with its mouth open, it looked like he was cooling off. She pointed him out to me. I couldn't believe we were on that little boat, completely overloaded with people. I prayed we'd make it to the other side alive. I remember how suddenly the feelings in my body collided. I didn't know whether to laugh or cry watching the gator on the sandbank who slowly turned around into our direction.

We were lucky; maybe he thought there were too many people in that boat, or maybe his appetite was not big enough early this morning. I was shaken up, but we reached the other side. I don't remember how long the trip took. We got out of the boat and walked for two hours through the rain forest to a bus station. From there we took the bus, which we changed three or four times that day until the coyote got us to our destination. A tiny town on the border of Mexico.

There was a little hotel, where we were instructed to stay put and wait for the right time and the right people to start the main part of our journey, crossing the border into Chiapas and up through Mexico to the border of the United States. The coyote who transported us here left us here, going back to El Salvador.

INTO CHIAPAS

We had to stay in this place for five days. My mother and I shared a little room. Lucky me I got my menstruation there; at least I got this out of the way. The money my mother payed in San Salvador was for the whole journey: hotel stay, meals, and transport included. The food was average, two meals a day, local food like tacos, soups, and tamales. The main man who ran this underground train was, to our surprise, a padre from a nearby church. When we saw the padre for the first time, we thought he wanted us to pray for a save journey, but it turned out that he was the chief organizer. He introduced himself and we could see from our room that there was preparation on the way, people coming and going.

In the evening of the fifth day, we were called into the main room. There we were briefed about the route. They wanted us to memorize certain details. Then, the padre introduced us to the coyotes who were supposed to get us all the way to northern Mexico. There were three of them. The main coyote for the journey was the padre's son. He had straight black hair, black eyes, was about 5'7" tall and skinny. Besides my mom and me, there were three other men waiting to be transported too.

We had to memorize the names of the coyotes and the three man: Carlos, Renee, and Leon. The padre also told us for this first part of the journey to wear shorts and dress, like the other girls and ladies in the area, not to attract attention. There was no marked borderline between Guatemala and Mexico, the area is mountain with rain forest, dirt roads, and paths cutting through it. At 11:00 a.m. we left the hotel by bus and headed to the padre's house. Here they made their final preparation for the journey, besides moving us north, every coyote had to transport a package from the padre, my mom found out later that there were drugs in these packages.

Everyone got a list with phone numbers to call, in case we got lost or separated. They wanted us to start out at three o'clock in the morning and prepared us for very long first day, therefore we had to get as much sleep as possible. With the coyotes we were eight people; it was three o'clock in the morning and still dark, when we left the padre's house in a four-wheel drive car, for the border, my mom, me and six men. For seven hours we drove on dirt roads, through mountains and valleys, covered by rain forest. We parked the car at a little farmhouse outside a small town, the coyote arranged a three-wheel minibus type of taxi, to get uss through that town without being stopped at any police checkpoints, now we were somewhere in Chiapas, Mexico, so they told us.

The taxi bus got us through, without any holdups and dropped us off on the side of the road, well outside town. The lead coyote told us to walk. We had to hold hands; that way it looked like a family walking home from town. We walked for about one hour until we reached a bus station. It was already afternoon. Finally, after another hour of waiting, we were able to board a bus. We were on this bus for about six hours until we reached a little hotel on the side of the road, where we got off and finally, could rest for the night. It was a long day and we were tired.

We used the hotel to stay, to clean ourselves up, and to get breakfast. It was a very long first day but at least we reached Mexico. The next morning, the main coyote arranged another taxi to get us into a side road, but the road was so bad, that the taxi had to drop us off halfway. We had to walk the rest of the way. After about one hour, there was a farmhouse which functioned as a way station for the coyotes, on the way north. There were four motorbikes, the main coyote took one bike with my mom. She had to sit behind and hold on to him.

We were the second bike. My coyote told me to put my arms around him and hold on as hard as I could, because this path was bad and he wanted to make sure that I am not falling down. He was short man, about 5'4", chubby, about 160 pounds with curly hair and very black eyes. The main coyote, who was ahead with my mom, knew the path through the rain forest. It was wet, slick and dirty, but he had used it before. We followed behind, followed by Carlos with the third bike and the third coyote.

This coyote was 5'7" tall and a very strong looking person with about 145 pounds. Renee and Leon followed last with the fourth bike. Renee had brown hair, skinny, 5'8" tall with yellow, brownish eyes and light skin. He was driving the motorbike, Leon was the smallest with 5'4" and about 140 pounds he was at the back seat.

Mom and the lead coyote got through, but the noise of the motorbike must have alerted the police, and we got caught. It was in the middle of the forest. They called in another police car, then they instructed us to follow them to an open place in the forest. I had to wait in the car, but before they took the coyote, he instructed me to say that all the stuff he had was my mom's, if they ask. They took the coyote over to another police car and stripped him completely naked on the side of the road, then they searched his clothes.

These policemen were not interested in us or any documentation; following their conversation they wanted money from the coyote. For these policemen, to shake down a coyote, was a possibility to make extra money and confiscate drugs, which they then sold to other narco traffickers. I followed the conversation as well as I could. The coyote kept cool. He had instructions what to say and do. I was scared to death, alone in this rain forest, with these strange men. My mother must have been hours ahead by now, and she did not know where I was.

I wondered where the other coyote was, who followed behind, leading the three other people. I did not know what to do. Should I try to run away? Maybe I could get back to the place where these policemen caught us and follow the path. With luck I maybe could meet up with the other coyote and the two motorbikes behind, but if I missed them, I could get eaten by some wild animal. I decided to stay put; walking alone through the rain forest was not an option. Hopefully my mom waited, wherever she was.

The argument between the guards and the coyote went on. It was a strange sight. He was completely naked arguing with them; finally they got all the money he had on him, as well as the motorbike and the package with the drugs. Lucky me, they were not interest in me, they gave him back his clothes, without the money and other valuables and let us go. They got what they wanted, but we had to walk. The place where they released us was far from the path we had followed. We did not know where we were, and we had to try to find the others.

The other coyote behind us must have realized that we got caught and decided to stop their noisy motorbikes and instead continued by walking. I don't remember how long we walked, but the coyote behind us, with Carlos, Renee, Leon were somehow able to meet up with us. I felt kind of relieved, but where was Mom? The two coyotes never went this route before. We were lost. They only had an idea of the general direction. We kept walking.

After hours of walking, suddenly out of nowhere, my mom and the lead coyote came back. He had used this path before and used the motorbike to move around, checking all the roads and paths in the rain forest. This was how they found us. My mother cried with relief. I was crying too; we were tired, wet, and hungry, but we had each other again. The main coyote decided to drop his motorbike too. We had to move silently, not get the police on our heels again. All our belongings we had left, we carried on us and in our backpack. The main coyote instructed us, to run and hide in the brushes, in case the police catch up with us. After several hours of walking, we reached the location where we should have checked in seven or eight hours before.

This station was a place in the middle of the rain forest. It had a simple roof, no walls, a bench to sit on, and a table. There was a fireplace to warm ourselves and cook a meal, there were no beds, instead there were hanging mats to sleep in. The toilet was a hole dug in the ground and a tree branch to sit on. It was a primitive place, but at least we stayed out of the rain, which started around midnight and it kept raining the whole next day. We were supposed to reach this place and continue by bike, but now we had to move on walking.

In the morning, we started walking to the next way station. It took us eight hours in the rain, but we reached it. It was almost identical to the place the night before. We were completely wet and the clothes in our backpack were wet too. This night was worse than the night before: we were wet, freezing, and hungry. All eight of us hunkered down as close to the fireplace as we could, to warm ourselves and dry the wet clothes. We all had a hard time relaxing under these circumstances and sleeping in this hanging mats was not easy, at least not comparable with sleeping in a bed, but it was the only way to avoid, snakes, mice, and other natural inhabitants of the rain forest's floor, that would possibly visit us at night and take a bite out of us. In addition, the smoke from the fire kept the flies, mosquitos, and the wild animals of the rain forest at bay.

The main coyote tried to get connection from his cell phone by climbing a tree on the highest spot in the area. After about an hour, he came back and said that he was able to arrange a pick-up in the next morning, but we had to walk to the meeting point. We started early and after several hours walking a tiny path, we reached a road where we had to wait. Finally, after about another hour, a pickup truck showed up. In the bed on the back he had a big tarp, he instructed us to climb in and hide under it. After more than two days walking through the rain forest, sleeping in hanging mats, and being around the smoke of the fireplaces during the night, we smelled like... I don't know, very stinky.

But when we crawled under the tarp of this truck it was obvious, this truck carried pigs and most likely unloaded them just before loading us up. It was obvious we would stink even more, as we were already. The main coyote took it with a smile, looking at us and said: "The police know he is transporting pigs to the marked, they never stopped him, and as bad as we are already smelling, it cannot make us smell worse; it's impossible." It was true, no police stopped us, we passed several checkpoints, without problems.

This did not mean we were in the clear. There was another car following us, whether they knew the driver or our main coyote and wanted to shake him down for money, we did not find out, the driver speeded up and as bad as the road was, they could not catch up with us; they finally gave up, we got away.

He dropped us off at a river, we had to cross over. I had a bad feeling remembering the previous crossing with the overloaded boot and the gators waiting for an easy meal. But this time there were no gators and the waters were hardly moving, but the boat was bad and had no engine, it took us several hours to cross. After we finally crossed, somebody said we were now in the Mexican state of Oaxaca.

OAXACA

From the other side of the river we continued by bus for a couple of hours; then we walked, and after two more hours, we took the bus again. The coyote told us we have to do it to avoid police checkpoints. By the end of the day we reached a hotel. Finally, we could shower and avoided the looks and distancing moves, from other people, because of our nasty smell. I remember, in my mind, I didn't know what to prioritize more at that point, washing or eating.

We faced another problem—Carlos was throwing up. He had to lie down right after showering. Whether he was just tired or he got a cold I don't know. He was a tough and strong-looking guy, bald, with tattoos on his face, arms and chest, dark skinned, but he did not look very tough right now. My mom had some aspirin in her backpack, which she gave him. We could only pray that he got over it fast. We needed to continue our journey. After being finished with ourselves, we washed and dried our clothes as good as we could. We had to help with Carlos's clothes too, hoping he was going to get better pretty fast.

After these days, sleeping in a bed felt like paradise and when the coyote told us we had to board a train the next morning, it sounded as the worst part of our journey was maybe behind us.

I would have wished to stay longer in bed, but the main coyote wanted us on the way. It had rained the whole night, and it was still raining. He ordered us to take water and something to eat, because it would be a long ride. We got our things together and went out in the rain again. There were railroad tracks behind the hotel. It was a freight train and this was not an official stop, to take on passengers or goods, only service stops where the conductors checked on the train and used the restroom; they only stopped for a few minutes. We had to hurry to climb on top of the railcar, we had to help each other to get on top of the train, not to get separated in case the train started moving.

It was raining and slick, and it made it difficult to get to the top. The coyotes helped us up. They had to help Carlos too; he was still sick and upset about what we had to endure. The long trip took a toll on all of us over the last couple of days, but he blamed the coyotes that we got caught by the police and having to leave the bikes behind and having to walk for two days. The coyotes ignored him as good as they could and besides helping my mom and me, they had to get Renee and Leon up with the two other coyotes too. When we were finally at the top, we realized we were not alone, there was a long line of people already siting on the roof, the whole length of the train were people sitting and holding on, mostly to each other, maybe 200 or so. Later we found out the figure was close to 500 people; everybody was wet and miserable.

We spent long hours on the roof of this train, eating and drinking what we had with us, it was raining most of the time, and we were freezing. The low hanging branches from the trees beside the rail tracks, hit us from time to time and we had to hold on to each other tight, not to be thrown down. It was packed, we were scared, it was dangerous, we could not move, especially in the darkness of the night. At one point a branch had hit a woman and thrown her off the train. We heard her screaming, but when she hit the ground it was silent. Maybe she got killed. It was dark, and we could not see anything. The train did not stop and everybody was occupied with themselves.

The worst was the restroom situation, there was none, when we needed to relieve ourselves, I had to hold Mom and Mom had to hold me. It was dangerous and very embarrassing, for everybody, not only for us. The train stopped from time to time, when the conductors did their checkups, and the people on the rooftop used these stops, to get on or off, depending whether they had reached their destination. Many poor people in Mexico used these freight trains for a way of transportation.

We used these stops to stand up and stretch out. One time it stopped, there were people on the side of the tracks from a Humanitarian organization, who distributed food, water and blankets. The coyotes instructed Mom and me to rush down in a hurry to get food and water and up again, because women got preferred treatment and more supplies from them. We were afraid that the train could leave without us, but at this stop, the train driver gave us extra time, not getting separated from each other. It was interesting to recognize, that there were still people who cared, in this country too.

After about fifteen hours, we could not take it anymore. The main coyote was here before. There was a little station and a hotel close by. We got off and went to the hotel. We were completely worn out. We ate, showered, and slept. The next morning the coyote got us going again. This train ride moved us north at a fast pace and he said the next ride should get us to Monterrey. We went back to the tracks again. There the coyotes got us to climb another freight train. This train transported cement in railcars. We were looking for an empty car, and lucky us we found one. There were already people in this car, but we found space.

In this part of Central Mexico there was another danger, the countryside was controlled by the "Los Zetas," a cartel. This cartel had their own uniform. They looked like paramilitaries and are heavily armed, with machine guns. One of their many ways of making money is to board these freight trains. They know that there are people using these empty railcars for transportation and even if they are poor people, they still climb in and rob them of their belongings, sometimes they try to rape the girls or even kill them, to get what they want.

We decided that two of us had to be awake at all times, and mom and me had to sleep in the middle of our six men. Our bodies were still hurting from the day before. We realized how serious the situation was when all the others in this railcar participated in this kind of alert system, and we kept it going throughout the night. Somebody advised us to have cash handy, in case they board the train to hand it over, to get them satisfied and out, as fast as possible. There are many bad stories about how these cartels operate. They make their money from robbing, kidnapping, and blackmailing people, charging way tolls, and they kill without hesitation, if it serves their purpose. We were lucky, this time we got through without problems.

MONTERREY

This train got us all the way to Monterrey and closer to the border. From this train station we boarded a bus to a hotel, where we checked in, it was the last way station for the coyotes. Our coyotes had reached the end of their journey, that day they introduced us to a different coyote who was supposed to meet up with us and take over from here. We were covered in cement dust from head to toe, the main coyote insisted we shower and wash our clothes as good as possible, then dress up in our best clothes we had left, not to attract attention, because we were close to the border. The coyotes also delivered the packages they carried, which my mom found out one day to be full of drugs, to their designated recipient.

REINOSA

Now, we had a new coyote we had to depend on, he was a truck driver and he drove a really big truck with a trailer. The truck had a big cabin for long distance hauling. Behind the front row seats, for the driver and the passenger, there was a bed, we five where all squatted around the cabin for the length of the drive, which took about twelve hours. Then we were supposed to hit a main police checkpoint where they checked the paperwork for the load and the passengers, making sure everything was in order and in accordance to the paperwork.

These checkpoints were also supposed to make sure that these trucks are not smuggling people. The coyote who was also owner of the truck decided that the three guys had to walk around the checkpoint, he let them out and explained where to walk and how to meet up with us again, then he instructed me to lie down on the bed in the back and pretend I was sleeping. If the police asked, my mom had to say she was his spouse and I had to pretend to sleep. He was not afraid to get arrested, but if they find something wrong, or something they don't like, then they usually shake us down for money.

We were lucky, they stopped us but were only interested in the freight he was carrying and not in us. We continued to a truck stop. There we had to wait for our guys to catch up with us. It took them about two hours and they were wet and freezing, Carlos was shaken and pissed off, because some dogs were chasing them; Renee and Leon were running away and he had to fight them off, alone, in the dark. The guys were tired, hungry, and scared. We finally reached a warehouse, the driver arranged something to eat. There was no time to sleep; it was already morning.

This morning another coyote was scheduled to take over from the truckdriver. He showed up early. It was an older gentleman; I think he was about sixty-five years old. He instructed us that we had to walk to a minibus station with him. He instructed my mom to hold hands with one of the guys and he held my hand. He said I was supposed to be his girlfriend, but it rather looked like I was his granddaughter. He never let my hand go. He wanted that it looked like we were a big family. The rest of the guys had to walk very close to each other too.

At the minibus station, we boarded a little bus, which dropped us off at a bus station, where we took a regular bus for a couple of hours. He wanted us to sit in groups of two. He did all the talking, buying the bus fare and all. He didn't want us to talk to anybody, because our dialect was different from the local people. This way we did not attract attention. He started reading my hand, and after a while he started explaining to me that everything will go fine. At first I thought he wanted to keep me to relax and it was his way to calming me down, but when he started to tell me that he can see that I will graduate from high school and learning English very fast. I wondered whether he was serious, or maybe had a gift doing this kind of thing.

My mom was sitting two rows in front of us and after we went through the past couple of days, I was not afraid. He then continued telling me that I will have a good relationship with my dad and he will be proud of me. This really surprised me, because the relationship with my dad was never good, for many years, but he continued telling me that the relationship with my dad will grow and over time get close; it made me feel good. He insisted that I will be okay with all the things I will do, during this journey and all I had to face in the future.

With these words, he touched a sensitive point in my soul, because during the hardship of the past weeks it came clear to me, that I have to change. It was my behavior that forced my mom to make these dramatic decisions. She had to leave my sister behind, the whole family, the house, her job. Not only did it change my life, it turned my mother's life upside down. I could not allow this happen ever again. At this point in my life, the little bad girl, who triggered all this, was already fading, as a thing of the past.

Him reading of my hand, strengthened the belief in myself and when he continued saying that I will face many obstacles, but will overcome them and come out stronger, it touched me deeply. For a moment, in my mind I saw my sister and my grandma, like they were standing in front of me and I started crying. How could I be so childish to get messed up with this gangs and put our lives in danger? How could I be so stupid and evil? Whether it was for the experience of the last weeks or because I had to leave my sister behind, my mind had already changed. All I wanted for our future now was to be successful, to be a better me, study, work hard, and help my mother.

We reached the bus stop. It was in the town of Reinosa, where we left the bus still holding hands. From there we walked to a house where a different coyote would take over. He introduced us and we said goodbye to him. Before he let go of my hand, he gave me a hug and told me again not to worry; I will be okay. Then he said to everyone to take care and good luck.

LENTELS

The new coyote never told us his name. At that point we were used to it because all coyotes we met were carefully giving their names, or at least their full names, but he made a point introducing himself by saying: "Guys, at this place you are going to be treated the way you treat us, if you don't respect us we don't respect you. If you acting up or give us problems, we make you disappear. And you women, if you want us to respect you, then respect yourself. Otherwise we will take advantage of you." I still remember the smile in the face of the coyote's girlfriend when she added, that there is a truck stop close by, the two girls who came through here two months ago still working the truck drivers to get the money for the border crossing.

This meant we could end up as prostitutes if we don't follow their rules. The coyote added that this is the way it will be: the time you spend here, you will help with cooking and cleaning. You boys I have some cleaning to do for you around the house. At that point my mom and me were glad that we had Carlos, Renee, and Leon with us, because this coyote and his girlfriend were scary. As difficult as Carlos was, his appearance could be intimidating, which was definitely good for us in this situation.

We soon realized that this coyote made a living of smuggling drugs, people, and forced girls and women to work as prostitutes for him if they were vulnerable.

We had to stay in this house for five days and it were fearful days; we had to sleep on the floor. We got one blanket, each of us. We got two meager meals a day, always a little bit rice, lentels and cactus, sometimes an egg. One day they gave us only a little soup of lentels, nothing else and I got sick. My stomach could not take it anymore. We were out of medication living with people who were only interested to get as much money out of us as possible, and I was throwing up, had diarrhea, and a temperature.

The second day the coyote asked Mom and our boys for the payment, to get us over the border, he said he will use the help of another coyote for the actual crossing. The charge was $1,200 per person crossing, and he said that they are ready to move in a couple of days, but he will not move us to the border before getting the money. My mom said she will see what she can do. We were already close to the border and my mom prayed that I got better fast, to finish our journey together and not being forced to stay behind alone with these dangerous people. My mom helped with the cooking, cleaned the house, and did the dishes. I remember, seeing the coyote and his wife getting in the shower together every night. The shower was right in front where we slept. It was annoying. They did whatever they did in the shower without shame or respect for us. We could not even sleep; they were too loud.

I wondered what my mom had in mind, how to get the money, but that night, when the coyote was in the shower playing with his girlfriend, she turned over and told me to watch them, and tell her if they got out; then she took my rubber band from my hair. I carried the band to hold my hair all the way from San Salvador, now I realized why she always paid close attention to it during the whole trip. The rubber band had money inside a lot of money, over $3,000. She took the $2,400 and put it into her bra to have it handy, the rest of the money she put back. Renee realized what my mom did, and he woke up the other two and they got moving fast too and pulled money from different parts of their clothes and their shoe's. Then everybody went back to sleep or pretend to sleep.

I remembered when we were in the hotel in Guatemala and the padre talked to my mom, that the money he charged there, is for the trip up to the border of the United States, for the crossing we will be charged separate by the people who organize and execute the crossing, so mom and the boys were prepared for that.

THE LAST COYOTE

The next morning, it was day four and the coyote told us that we will leave the next morning. This morning a new person showed up. It was another coyote. The first thing they wanted was to get paid. My mom handed over the money for me and her, she got our boys to watch it, when they counted it and we watched the payment Carlos, Renee, and Leon made for them.

We were lucky, or God was with us, one or the other, I got better, just in time, when this coyote got ready to move. It was the last coyote. We left this scary house in separate pickup trucks. All the guys in one truck, and my mom and me in the other. At that point we did not know that this was the last time we saw Carlos, Renee, and Leon. The coyote planned a separate crossing area for the guys. We never could say goodbye to them and it makes me still sad today, that we could not see them again, ever. We trusted each other especially in the last part of the trip. Carlos had his temper and his outbursts but was always good to us. He was a strong-looking, and tough guy, not even the crazy coyote with his equally crazy girlfriend messed with him, which helped us a lot. Now we were alone, I was scared to dead. Instinctively my mom and me held on to each as close as we could.

We got dropped off at a house. There were other people already waiting to be crossed too. There were women and children sleeping on the floor, on smelly old mattresses. There was another mother and her son from El Salvador there, the boy was maybe seven or eight years old and the coyote put us together with her and two other girls, he planned to cross us together. This Coyote owned several houses where he stashed people to get them ready for crossing.

We had reached the final part of our long journey, and I realized the attention this coyote payed to us, or as I soon to find out to my mom. I appreciated the extra food, after we were starved for days, but when he invited my mom to walk with him, I started wondering. He had a two-year-old son and whether he was a widower or divorced, we did not find out, but he wanted my mom to stay.

At one point, when I was asleep, my mom left, I woke up and she was gone. I was very concerned almost panicked, but finally after about two hours, she came back. I waited for her. My mom had a long talk with him and politely made him understand that after all we went through, she was not willing to stop here at the border and be a mother to his two-year-old son. She had me to take care off and after the rough journey we had behind us, we wanted to finalize it and get to the United States, not settle down here, right at the border.

RIO GRANDE

Finally, he accepted our wish and that morning, he told us to get our things together. I remember we were eating breakfast with our backpack, ready to go. We got into his pickup Truck, together with the other mom and her little son, as well as to the other girls in their twenties, we left from the Rio Grande. On the riverfront, there was a man waiting, it was somewhere between Reynosa and Matamoros.

He wanted us to cross the border here, in a small boat with oars, with all six of us and him in the boat. He told us to take off all our earrings, rings, and other metals, because on the other side of the river it is the United States. There where sensors and metal detectors that capture any type of metals.

He also said, when we reach the other side to get some rocks, in case we stepped on snakes or other animals to throw rocks at them and try to get them away. At that point you are already in the United States.

We got into the boat. The Rio Grande was calm on this place and we got over easily. He let us off and we stepped on land and into the USA. He said to keep walking, immigration would find us one way or the other. We looked around, not sure in what direction to go; for the first time we were without a coyote to tell us what to do and where to go. We had a little bottle of water left, which we shared between us, then started walking away from the river. We remembered what the man told us and we hoped not to step on any snakes or other animals. We walked for about one hour, not knowing where we were or where to go, then my mom remembered about the sensors the coyote was talking about and she pulled her earrings out and put them on again, together with her ring, I did the same.

JOHANN STIRNER AND DIANA BERRIOS REYES

DETENTION

After another fifteen minutes walking, we realized that somebody was following us. We were afraid. We were only women and children. At first, we thought it is maybe somebody who was trying to rob us, so we grabbed some rocks and stones to defend us if necessary. Then the lady who walked with her son called, "Who is there? Come out of the bushes." He came out. It was a Border Patrol Agent recording us. He had followed us for a while. We dropped the rocks we had collected to defend ourselves and started crying. He directed us to walk with him and after a couple of minutes we were surrounded by immigration officers with cars and even a helicopter was above us.

We all were very nervous and crying, then one of the officers brought us a bottle of water and a burrito for each of us. We were so nervous that we could not eat or drink, they put us in a patrol car and drove us to a border station. We had to wait there for about a half hour; then we had to board a minibus that transported us to a detention center. It was about 1:00 p.m. when they separated us. My mom was taken to a cell with the women, and I was put in a cell with the children. There were fifteen other children there besides me. I was the oldest. The youngest child looked like four years old. They could only see their moms by looking out the window in our cell and many where crying. I felt terrible being alone in this naked cell. After a while I thought to myself that these children must feel worse. They were younger than me and their moms were locked up in the same room my mom was. These children looked lost and most of them were crying. Some of them played. I did not know when it was the last time they were allowed to see their mothers. The cell had one toilet and a sink. We had to sit and sleep on the naked concrete floor. It was very cold, and we did not have blankets. Instead they gave us aluminum foil to stay warm; it looked like and felt like jail.

On the other side of the building was my mom's cell. She was held there with the other mothers. We could only look over when we stayed at the window. To see my mom like this and not being able to be with her or at least talk to her made me cry too. It was hard. I could only imagine how the other children must have felt. I could see through the window that she had tears running down her chicks. I went to the back of the cell and sat down on the floor. I was hungry, freezing, and wanted to be with my mom. I stayed there for about two hours feeling miserable, between all the other crying and freezing children, some of them killing time by playing.

Some of them lay down side by side, as close as possible to each other, to keep warm and try to sleep. In the night when the children were asleep, I found an empty spot beside them, and I lay down too. We got some sleep by warming each other. At five o'clock they gave each of us a burrito and a bottle of water. It was the smallest burrito I ever saw.

As I heard from my mom later, the situation was similar with the women in their cell. They missed their children, had also very little to eat, and the same aluminum foil to stay warm. My mom shared her burrito with a pregnant woman in her cell. When she could not see me through the window anymore, she was thinking that I was sleeping. She tried to sleep too, leaning against the window with her aluminum foil around, in case I woke up and was looking for her. This was a terrible and lonely night, thinking about my mom, hearing the other children sobbing, crying, asking for their mothers, freezing, using the toilet.

The next morning the guards woke us up at five in the morning, each of us got another mini burrito. Some of the kids started playing, some started crying again. I could not cry anymore. There was a little kid beside me asking for his mom. I hugged him and told him that his mom was across the room in the other cell. We tried to look, but we could not see her and we did not know where she was. At noon they gave us a sandwich and a bottle of water. I stood at the window, looking for my mom. She was there. I was so relieved to see her and waved my arm to show her that I was okay. She did not have her aluminum foil anymore. She told me later that she gave it to a pregnant woman who was trembling and freezing. At 5:00 p.m. they gave us the last meal of the day, another mini burrito, that's all we ate.

I heard later that the adults ate the same as us. When they brought us our meals, my mom asked the guard for some extra food and a blanket for the pregnant woman who was with her in the cell. She asked the guard whether they could set the air-conditioning higher, but they said they had to keep it at the level as the temperature in the hospitals to avoid bacteria to spread. The guard came back with a blanket and an extra sandwich for the pregnant woman and my mom. My mom was still not able to sleep that night. She was cold and could not stop thinking about me.

Finally, the next morning they let my mom out of the cell for questioning. She was sitting on the bench waiting and we could look at each other, through the window, I felt relieved to see her, the border guard wanted to know her contact in the United States, if she had one. My mom gave them the phone number from her sister, my aunt, who lives in Houston. One half hour later, they let me out of my cell to be with my mom. I ran over to her and started crying; my mom too.

It was the first time I saw her crying like this. I felt my heart pumping. She said she was sorry; she never wanted to put me in a situation like this. I told her it was not her fault; it was mine. I was the reason for this journey. We did not know what was going to happen next, and we got no information from the guards.

My mom continued saying, "Diana, if we have to go back, I will never want you going through this ever again." I told her to never mention this ever again, and we hugged each other.

My aunt sent the money for the bus fare the same day. We had to sign some papers and got released in the afternoon. A taxi got us to the bus station. The taxi driver gave the bus driver the address and asked him, kindly to dropped us off at the nearest bus stop. The bus ride to Houston took six hours. My aunt waited already at the bus stop, and we had reached our destination. It took us twenty-two days.

A NEW BEGINNING

The first days went by, eating and sleeping. My aunts, cousins and the rest of the family were happy that we were alive and made it. Now we were reunited, even if we had nothing left but the clothes on our body and the shoes we were wearing. My aunt bought us clothes, shoes, and what we needed. Now my mom had to get a job and I had to start school.

We were here, but we were not able to get legalized. When we were in custody at the Border Patrol, they checked on my mom, and they could see in the computer that my mom had requested a visa several times for me, my sister, and her. The embassy in El Salvador filed the paperwork but never granted it because my mom was a certified nurse, employed by the hospital, which is a government job. Furthermore, she owned a house and my sister and me went to private school. What the files in the computer did not show were the circumstances which led to the desperate decision for our journey, no word about the threat to our lives from the gangs.

When we tried to explain, they did not believe us. They just laughed at us and said this is just one of the stories everybody from Central America comes up with. They had heard it many times. I got angry when they laughed at us; I almost cussed at the officer, but my mom stopped me, and without the officer noticing too much, she calmed me down. After all we had to go through, it made me mad that this officer could say everybody coming from Central America is lying. At least they did not deport us. We got fingerprinted and signed some paperwork, before they released us into the custody of my aunt.

We lived with my aunt's family for eight months in Houston, Texas, but it was not possible to get work there, my dad finally stepped up and told us to move to California. It is easier to get a job there without papers; he also got me into school there. So, we started to prepare to move. During these months, I was very happy playing with my aunt's dog. Her name was "Chica." She had curly hair. After six months, Chica got puppies. She had six of them and I decided to adopt one of them. It was the one, who was different-looking. He had four different colors. He was beautiful: black, white, brown, and yellow. For our remaining time in Texas, I took care of all the puppies. My aunt kept one; the remining four we gave away. Then the time came to move. My dad had found a place for us to live.

My aunt and the rest of the family was sad, but we had to move on and make the best out of the situation. My aunt was concerned to transport the puppy with us, because we had to go through an Agricultural Checkpoint. You cannot bring seeds, fruit, and fresh food. She was concerned that they could put "Sonny," this is how I named him, in quarantine or worse put him to sleep. They are very strict at these checkpoints. We thought about it for a while, but one way or the other, we did not want to lose him. We decided to take a chance and hide him before we reached the checkpoint.

When we went on our road trip "Sonny" was so small and tired that he slept behind the driver seat and did not make any noise. When they stopped us at the checkpoint and asked us whether we had any fruit, seeds, or animals, we said no, they went back and checked the bed of the truck, then they let us go. Now we were in California. I went to high school got my diploma, went to college and now I'm sitting here waiting for the mechanic to finish.

LUNCH TRUCK

The little pretty lady with the name Diana looked at me and said: "Sir, this is my story. It was a difficult journey." I did not know what to answer. I could not even say anything, I was speechless.

Anyway, the mechanic had arrived one hour ago, whatever was wrong with her lunch truck, he fixed it and got it started. She smiled at me and said, "Thank you" and left.

EPILOGUE

After World War II, the United States was the live boot and island for millions of people who had lost everything, even their countries. They had a plan, a "Marshall Plan" (named after Secretary of State and former General "Marshall"—The Marshall Plan was an economic assistance program, which helped Western Europe's economic recovery after the second World War.) It helped, educated, defended people, and rebuilt their countries. It promoted and installed, liberty, democracy, freedom, and hope.

Today the US is seen by many as looking only out for itself. Its southern neighbors fighting gangs, drugs, cartels, while they try to improve the living conditions of their people. The law enforcement in these countries is weak and overwhelmed, often they are corrupt. The money payed for these drugs comes from the United States, its biggest market, but it is also the one country who offers liberty, freedom, prosperity, and respect for the law, which makes it a magnet for the people from these countries, for too many the only way to escape these conditions. For some they desperately try to make the journey north.

Efforts like the creation of "NAFTA helped, but by itself it's not enough, because it doesn't resolve their need for security and political stability. The people in these countries not only need to be moved into the free market system, but also help to improve law and order, strengthen their democracies and the transfer of power. Help and assistance is desperately needed. The politicians in Washington should pay more attention to what is happening on its front door, instead some of them defend their passivity behind the argument that the US isn't good in "Nation Building," maybe, because so far they were unable to improve the situation in these countries, right at their front door.

El Salvador, Honduras, and Guatemala, are together about the size of California, both in square miles, as well as their population. Europe was a continent with different languages and nations. This three countries are not far behind Puerto Rico, in language and education, but in this situation, the United States appears clueless, no plan is on the table to turn these countries into a zone of opportunity, develop their economy, improve their education, and push the political leaders in these countries to turn it into a zone of law and order, similar as the US did in Western Europe after World War II.

Only with the help and guidance of the United States, can these countries strengthen their institutions and improve their economies so the caravan of people leaving can be slowed down, but Washington chooses to sit on the sideline. The politicians seem trapped in bickering and complaints about these Central Americans, invading the border and taking jobs away from the US citizens.

DIANA R· - MY JOURNEY

AUTHOR: Johann Stirner   Email: johannstirner@outlook.com

CO-AUTHOR: Diana Reyes   Email: diana9167@hotmail.com